DOING THE WORK
WHILE WAITING

A Singles Workbook

TANYA MARAYNE

AREA UNDER
CONSTRUCTION

Introduction

I remember watching the sitcom "Living Single" in my earlier years. The show was about the challenges of being single. I remember thinking about how all the women were beautiful, educated, and independent. So were the men. I would often think to myself; *why are they still single?* Why am I still single? Dang! Some of us are asking ourselves this question right now.

I created this workbook specifically for individuals who may feel excluded or unsure about how to begin preparing for a relationship. We often hear some say, "Love yourself, prepare for your mate, and even go as far as to say that all you need is God." Their comments make some of us singles feel bad for wanting marriage. If God did not want marriage, He would not have said in *Genesis 2:18 (KJV)* that it was not good for man to be alone.

Today, I pray for all the single men and women who desire to get married, that any negative thoughts or opinions may not influence them. I intercede on our behalf to help us gain confidence in knowing God loves us. He has not forgotten about us. He has us on his mind. Let this workbook serve as a source of wisdom, knowledge, guidance, and encouragement as we embark on the journey of finding our mate or being found by them. Let's get that drive rooted deep down inside and pursue the benefits God has for us while doing the work on ourselves.

TABLE OF CONTENTS

PART ONE

GIFT, ACCEPTANCE, CARING FOR THE THINGS OF GOD

Chapter 1
A Gift

Let me start off by saying "God loves you" and don't you ever forget it. No matter what is going on around you, remember, He cares for you. To prepare for this workbook, research revealed an article of how the church has been slothful in its attentiveness to the trials and needs of single men and women *(Hsu, 2022. p. 2)*. In fact, the article highlights that many believers are not convinced that a church should allocate resources to ministering to singles. The writer further stated that most believe it is "more Christian" to be married than to be single *(Hsu, 2022, p. 1)*.

In continuation, the article noted that the Old Testament times viewed being unmarried as unnatural and unwanted *(Hsu, 2022, p. 1)*. Unwanted. Wow. Yes, I am bothered by those findings as you are right now. Thus, I wanted to search God's word to see what He thought about the single individual. I can remember growing up in my twenties and having friends that received pressure from family members and society to get married and have babies. Young men and women were getting married just because, or because they did not want to sin by having sexual relationships before marriage and reasons for the title, others because of the so-called biological clock.

Lord, have mercy. I did not want that kind of pressure. In today's time, the Holy Spirit must lead us before we enter any type of relationship. The enemy loves to cause chaos in marriages because he dislikes unity. There is nothing wrong with waiting and I can attest waiting was not my strong point, which made my lessons even harder in life. In fact, revelation has made known to me there is nothing wrong with me because I am not married. There is no condemnation of being single. The scripture is our back up as it states in *(Romans 8:1a)* that there is no condemnation to them which are in Christ. He loves us so much that he gave his only son that whoever believes in him will not lose their life but will have eternal life. Isn't the gift of life more important?

God values the lives of all individuals, regardless of their gender or marital status. However, I want to highlight an observation I have made over the years. Women get a lot of attention. There is so much attention placed on their hurt, pain, selfishness, and their need for companionship. But what about our male counterparts? God considers the needs of single men too, and there are men who desire marriage as well. Some of them have also experienced hurt and endured suffering in silence. Ladies, our brothers should not need to feel devalued or counted as non-important in the singles equation. Men's voices need to be heard. A good deal of men suffer silently in their struggles to maintain respect and dignity as a single individual. The world stripped them of so much until they began to act out of character. To lead or not to lead, to be chivalrous or not to be. If they give a female a compliment, insecure women immediately join the cause and claim to have joined the "me too" movement. All he is doing is being courteous. Many women mistakenly assume that if a man is single, there must be something wrong with him.

God is no respecter of persons. In simpler terms, this workbook will bring blessings to our brothers as well. There needs to be a release in the atmosphere for our men to be free from condemnation when his choice is to be single. He needs to know God remembers him. *(Psalm 136:23)*

(Isaiah 56:4-5) highlights that eunuchs who faithfully serve the Lord, follow His ways, and choose to please Him will not be cut off and their names would be everlasting. So, if God said Eunuchs will not cut off, then we can rest assure God will keep his word for us.

My Father in Heaven will not forget about the man who is single. It was surprisingly revelatory in the piece written by *Hsu (2022, p. 2)* that in the Old Testament, the only way to eternal life is to have family who remember you and carry your name. But our God is a God who remembers us all. My sisters, please don't be upset with me. I just want to capture the needs of both single men and women in this workbook and took a brief look at the men first. Let's look at what Paul writes in (*1 Corinthians Chapter 7*) about the unmarried.

In (*1 Corinthians 7:7*), Paul writes he wishes for us to be as he is, which is single, but he also understood everyone has one grace to be this or the other. The scripture reads according to the NIV version of The Women's Study Bible (2018), "But each of you has your own gift from God". God has graced us to be in whatever state we desire. Whether to remain single or married. There is a positive here in that no matter what position the single man or woman chooses, God loves us either way. We should not govern our singleness by the world's standard but govern our minds by transformation using God's word and will for us as individuals. You can find this reference in the book of (*Romans 12:2*).

Therefore, once we renew our minds with the word of God, we can view our single status as a gift. We were all made in his likeness, in his image male and female, and God blessed us with dominion. (*Genesis 1:26-27*). Hsu (2022) says it well. "Would it be acceptable to give a gift back or exchange a gift"? How would the giver feel if you gave them their gift back? Maybe that you are being ungrateful?

Look at it this way, single people, there is nothing hindering us or restricting our progress. We are free to explore interests such as going back to school, traveling, or even pursuing a new career goal. Ladies, that dress you saw at Nordstrom for $500 will have a mate looking at you with a side eye, however when you are single, you are free to spend your own money. I would hope wisely, but at any rate, you got it like that. And let's not forget my brothers, who purchase $1000 rims a pop. Your wife could have thought of other ways to use that money. My point is whether someone is single or married, we can find freedom and salvation through Jesus Christ, which is also a gift of God, eternal life. Hallelujah.

The best thing about being in Christ is that when one does marry, it only means that one gift is being exchanged for another *(Hsu, 2022, p. 4)*. What an interesting way to look at our singleness as a gift.

Scripture Reference

"For I would that all men were even as I myself, But every man hath his proper gift of God, one

after this manner and

another after that."

1 Corinthians 7:7 (NIV The Woman's Study Bible)

Let's Work it Out!

1. After reading Chapter One, what is the main idea you received about how God views singleness? What does this mean for your life?

_____

_____

_____

_____

_____

_____

_____

_____

_____

_____

_____

_____

2. What ways can you think of to renew your mind when it comes to your single state of life? After renewal of your mind, your view of your singleness should change.

_____

_____

_____

_____

_____

_____

3. After reading this scripture, how do you feel about your single state? What is more important? (*Romans 6:23*).

_____

_____

_____

_____

_____

_____

4. Outside of church, what other interests would you like to explore? What steps are you taking to explore those interests?

_____

_____

_____

_____

_____

_____

5. What have you failed to take dominion over in your life today while waiting for your

mate?

_____

_____

_____

_____

_____

_____

6. Take a moment to reflect on what "a gift of exchange" truly means to you?

_____

_____

_____

_____

_____

_____

_____

_____

_____

_____

_____

7. For individuals aged sixty and above, what advice would you like to give to the younger generation regarding being unmarried, divorced, or widowed? Write your Notes:

_____

_____

_____

_____

_____

_____

_____

_____

_____

_____

_____

Chapter 2
Acceptance

Have you ever thought of how you would feel if you were never to marry? God mentioned it was okay to be single if one can accept it. *(Matthew 19:11)* It would be of great consequence to live and rejoice in whatever state you find yourself in *(Philippians 4:11)*. If an individual is not graced with the gift of marriage, just know that it is possible to live a life of great abundance and grace through God, who strengthens us to do so *(Philippians 4:13)*. Life is not guaranteed; in fact, the word of God describes life as a vapor. Live life to the fullest so that there is no regret.

I need to be transparent with you. I was involved in a toxic relationship, and I stubbornly refused to acknowledge the fact that it was never meant to be. The harder I tried, the worse the disrespect and abuse became. I repeated this cycle over and over while dating. The treatment I received pushed me back into the arms of my very first love, God the Father, Son, and Holy Ghost. There was an immediate revelation needed in this instance to accept the fact those relationships were not God sent. I realized I was better off without those relationships. Whether or not it's love, toxicity remains nothing but poison. The consumption of poison destroys you from the inside out.

Finally, I walked away for the last time, and it was a struggle. The enemy desires to keep us bound in these poor relationships, thinking that we can choose better than God can. The enemy wants to trap you in the relationship where you will become so consumed that you forget about your Heavenly Father, who cares for you. Remember how Eve was deceived in the garden of Eden? That's what it looks like when we think we can choose better than God can. Let's not deceive ourselves just because we desire something so bad, knowing it is not good for us. Many of us right now, while reading this book, know for sure you are in a relationship you need to get out of, for it's a matter of life and death. God already showed you and warned you. It is an ungodly soul tie. Do you not understand that when someone unites with a prostitute, their bodies become one, as mentioned in (*1 Corinthians 6:16*)? Escaping from this type of hold requires the help of the Holy Trinity: God the Father, Son, and Holy Spirit. "But whosoever is united with the Lord is one with him in spirit" (*1 Corinthians 6:17*). Recognize that all things are possible when you rely on Christ's empowerment. Prepare yourself to get out of it now. Withdrawal are normal parts of the process, so pay attention and be aware. Keep pushing and accept the fact that some things are just not meant to be. Listen, God is all knowing and all seeing. He saw ahead of time what that person was going to do to you. In my case, God fixed it so no matter how much love I showed this guy, the more he rejected it, it was like a plague to him. He did not want it. He wanted to stay in his misery because, guess what? He was not healed himself. We all know the saying "hurt people, hurt people." Take a pause right here and let God minister to you about your current situation-ship, condition-ship or no-ship, meaning you don't know what it is. Right now, let God minister to you and heal you, because it's time to release that dreadful thing. Allow God to guide you towards the good thing and the good thing can be found.

Accept God's love toward you. There are benefits to loving God. He will never let you be in toxic relationships that can cause you harm. Once you get that revelation, another can never devalue you and cause doubt about where you stand with God. God doesn't bring confusion. That's the enemy's mode of operation.

In retrospect, this is the first time in my life that I am truly single. I'm not interested in just dating to be dating or having lengthy phone conversations that lead to nowhere. I am waiting to be found. Some time ago, I realized that there was a lot of personal work I needed to do. Wow, I thought. What would I do if God never sends my mate? Am I going to lie down and die, be content, or fight this tooth and nail? Well, sometimes you must talk to yourself as a reminder of what happens when you try to do things on your own?

Okay, so what am I saying? You really don't have a choice but to depend on God's instructions for your life. I pray for the reader to exercise being content in whatever position your life journey takes you. Warning! Denial will only cause bitterness, mean spiritedness and frustration trying to do it on your own. The one thing you don't want to do is resent God. Your singleness is not the end of the world and just because you are unmarried, that doesn't mean your life is meaningless. I must continue to emphasize this; you have meaning and are just as important to God as the married couple. I can surely attest that it gets lonely sometimes. However, when I think of my bad choices, I can certainly find it possible to wait on God for sure this time. Stay with me now. Just think of how long it took to get over that troubled relationship, only to jump into another unhealthy relationship, one after the other, slowly allowing the enemy to kill you on the inside. Remember, he comes to steal, kill, and to destroy. Agree with your single state for a while, gather your senses and think things through, pray and seek God's direction. A self-evaluation. Study yourself and produce a plan of do's, don'ts and won't. It is imperative to recognize bad choices and kill the root.

My brother and my sister, sometimes you need alone time to establish boundaries and truly take a step back to consider how much you have settled for in the past. Consider this: all this time, God had someone so much better for you. I find much peace in thinking about my present circumstances rather than dwelling on the painful relationships of my past. I can simply disregard his unruly behavior with no concern, and I don't have to let my days be disrupted because I didn't get a phone call from him. My brothers, you can now let go of the confusion of why she doesn't answer the phone or stress over trying to love someone. Only to find out later on that this entire time you're claiming them, and they have been publicly denying you.

Jesus is one man who will never forsake us or lie to us. Do you trust God today? Do you believe He is your strength, shield, and that He will help you? Will you allow your heart to trust him today? *(Psalm 28:7)* Remember, God will make all things beautiful in his time *(Ecclesiastes 3:11a)*. And in his time, He will do it quickly *(Isaiah 60:22)*. We have no clue what God is doing in our lives. However, the one takeaway I would like the reader to get from this is "Acceptance does not mean Restriction."

Scripture Reference

"... For I have learned to be content whatever the circumstances..."

Philippians 4:11 NIV The Women's Study Bible

Let's Work it Out!

1. How have you shown your contentment or discontentment in your single state? Have you become angry, impatient, or bitter? Explore this area in your life. Write them down to address them one by one.

_____

_____

_____

_____

_____

_____

2. List some ways to combat impatience, bitterness, and loneliness?

_____

_____

_____

_____

_____

_____

_____

3. After reading Chapter 2, what is the main takeaway for you to live a life of acceptance in whatever state you are in today? (list more if you need to)

_____

_____

_____

_____

_____

_____

4. What specific areas do you think you need to improve as an individual in order to become a better version of yourself?

_____

_____

_____

_____

_____

_____

_____

5. Finally, are you ready to walk away from what's hurting you? Why? How? Use scripture to help you deal with this question. This is your personal answer. Remember, you can do all things through Christ.

_____

_____

_____

_____

_____

_____

6. Fill in the blank: Acceptance does not mean _____.

If you are in your seasoned years of sixty and over, note challenges in accepting your single status and how have you overcome obstacles: divorce, widower, separated?

_____

_____

_____

_____

_____

_____

_____

Chapter 3
Caring for the Things of God

Serve the Lord with gladness come before his presence with singing. *(Psalm 100:2)*. Are you ready to serve? What is your worship and prayer life like? When is the last time you gave God a praise just for who he is? Have you discovered your God given purpose and gift for your life? What has God called you to do? What is your passion? If you know what that is, are you walking in it? Ask yourself what would I like to do whether I get paid for it or not? How does this fit into God's kingdom? Does this provide a solution to someone's problem?

Can God find you walking in your purpose? I remember when God called out and asked Adam, where are you? So, my question to you is where are you? God knew the answer. He just wanted Adam to be cognizant of his situation. God gave us all a purpose, whether single, married, divorced, or widowed. He who is unmarried cares for the things of the Lord and how to please him *(1Corinthians 7:32)*. Therefore, being single does not mean we just sit around and do nothing. There are so many ways to enjoy life and make it a great one if we would just focus on the gift giver than our present state. *(Galatians 5:13)* reminds us that we should not "use our freedom to indulge in the flesh but serve one another humbly in love."

I can remember the words of my previous pastor: "You have to be found in God to be seen." Well, what he meant is for some singles laboring for Christ is one way to be seen or found. Ponder a bit and ask yourself, are you a church visitor or an active member? Key word "active." What auxiliaries do you serve in your place of worship? Are you one of the ones that the follow up ministry must call every week to find out if you're going to show up for service on Sunday? Or are you just holding up the pew? If you remember in the previous chapters, there was a mention of singleness as a gift and accepting the will of God for your life. Well, serving God and his people are ways you accept God and enjoy your benefit of being one of his children. There is a special benefit of being single. Think freely.

Let me recommend a resource for you if you find it challenging to discover your purpose. This book "Discover Your God-Given Gifts" by Don and Katie Fortune is a useful tool to aid you in this challenge. The book details characteristics one may exhibit and gives the reader insight as to which gift it relates to. There may be one or several gifts, but the gift with the highest score usually reveals who you are, even without thinking about it. In your spare time, check it out.

Serve! Serve! Serve! "Just as the son of Man did not come to be served, but to serve and to give his life as a ransom for many *(Matthew 20:28)*. To the single man and woman let us take advantage of the time we have alone because once you get married, your entire focus changes from caring about the things of God to directing all your attention towards your spouse and the things of the world *(I Corinthians 7:32)*. Today, I encourage you to serve God with all your might before you get married, so that when your spouse comes, you will be so rooted in God. This way, there's no way you can lose yourself because you would have found your purpose and acceptance of God's love that will help you survive in your marital status. Jesus serves us in that he gave his life for us, rose again, now sitting on the right hand of the Father, making intercession for us.

Oh, my goodness, how great is our God! How merciful of a God we relate to. If God said we can cast our cares upon him because he cares for us, how could we, as individuals, neglect to care for the things concerning God's kingdom? One should serve because we love a God who first loved us. If we seek him first and his kingdom and his right ways, he will add all the other things to us *(Matthew 6:33)*. Serving should be done without murmuring and complaining *(Philippians 2:14)*. In fact, what if Jesus decided he did not want to take the cup of death for our sakes? Have you ever thought of where you would be? Saints of old would sing "father I stretch my hand to thee, no other help I know, if you withdraw, thou hand from me where would I go?

We serve because we love God and not just to be seen. However, how can we expect to be found in the right place at the right time if we are not seen? Remember Ruth? She was not a lazy woman who found her hands to be busy in a field where she was picking up leftovers. She was in the field of Boaz at the right time. When he saw her, keyword **saw**, he inquired, "who is that"? *(Ruth 2:5)*. Come on, fellas, you can relate when you see a woman of interest. "Who is that lady? Hallelujah. People, all it takes is to be in the right place at the right time, doing the work of the Lord! Serving the Lord has its rewards. If the story of Ruth does not get your feet moving and your spirit on fire, I don't know what else to tell you. Somebody needs to catch on fire with this! Let the Holy Ghost move right now on you. I dare you to just stop where you are and just give God a praise for your future. It's okay to praise God in advance. Sometimes you just need a praise break so all that heaviness can fall off.

"I would like you to be free from concern. An unmarried man is concerned about the Lord's affairs – how he can please the Lord. But a married man is concerned about the affairs of this world – how he can please his wife."

(I Corinthians 7:32-33)

Let's Work it Out!

1. What does serving the Lord look like to you in your everyday activities?

_____

_____

_____

_____

_____

_____

2. Ladies, what can you learn from Ruth? *(Ruth 2-3:18)*

_____

_____

_____

_____

3. Gentlemen, what can you learn from Boaz? *(Ruth 2-3)*

_____

_____

_____

_____

_____

_____

4. What choices can you make now regarding servanthood that will help you in your current or future relationship with others and/or potential spouse?

_____

_____

_____

_____

_____

_____

_____

5. Think of what solution can you provide for the kingdom of God's people? Write down your vision and how-to's in this section and then act on it. Pursue.

_____

_____

_____

_____

_____

_____

_____

_____

_____

_____

_____

_____

_____

_____

_____

_____

Chapter 4
What is Hindering You?

When I accepted the Lord Jesus Christ into my heart, I was about 19 years old. I stepped out of the pew, and I remember Sis Stephanie saying, "I will go with you." We walked to the front of the church and I repeated the sinners' prayer. Immediately, the Holy Spirit touched me, and I went down to the ground. I was with my family when I descended gracefully to the ground, and they became alarmed, assuming that something was wrong with me. But that was just the beginning of my Christian walk with Christ.

I was single as well in a relationship, but not married. I was also attending College towards a nursing degree. The gentleman I was dating at the time questioned me? The gentleman I was dating at the time questioned me, asking if I was sure I was saved. I had to call the Reverend and ask her if what happened today meant I was saved. Immediately, the enemy used my unsaved boyfriend to thwart my walk with God and cause me to question what took place. Granted, I was new and naïve to the challenges I would face, but there was just not enough solid teaching. There was no class or follow up to see if I had questions nor was there direction. Just church, Sunday school, bible study and many musicals. Singles need straight forward teaching and guidance, not rebuke. I had no clue what to ask, however, by and by, God's Will revealed itself to me. The rest was because of my rebellion and disobedience and thinking that being saved was no fun. This reasoning was so untrue. I just had not tapped into my purpose yet. As individuals, we have a responsibility for our own walk with Christ.

Therefore, to my single brother and sister, what is hindering you from serving God and giving your life to him? What tools do you need? Have you conferred with your pastor or pastors? Do you feel confident being truly transparent before them? Are you ready to live for Christ whole heartedly? I ask this because, for me, trust was one of my issues. Once I observed a first Lady, spilling all gossip about women in the church, my heart turned. Where are the true women of God? I asked? Why is she mentioning this to me? Her behavior let me know that if I had a struggle, she would not be the point of reference.

Many people have experienced hurt in the church; however, we also have experienced relationship hurt with that significant other as well. And we take them back several times. I mentioned this scenario because this may be something you've experienced in the past or even worse. This is the time to examine those instances and give it to the Lord for healing so that we are not stagnant in the things of God and be able to obtain what he has in store for us. My brothers and sisters, many of you have been waiting for a long time to either find a wife or have a husband find you. So let nothing get in the way of your relationship with God first! He is the most important one! If you must leave a church to be where God wants you to be, then do so. But do it decently. Don't badmouth the leadership, keep it to yourself and give that situation to God and at the right time, God will cause an opportunity for you to share with them your concerns. Don't carry around aught against anyone. Get that thing right with the person to free yourself to unlock your blessings that are waiting in heaven for disbursement to you on earth.

Permit me to bring another question to mind. How do you view your current relationship with the Lord? May I suggest taking some time to visit this area? There can be a misconception of what a relationship with God is. Some feel it is "give me" "give me." Is your praise and worship based on what he can give you? Have you asked yourself, do I really love the Lord, or do I just want the benefits he can give me without a relationship? Is it the house, the car, the degree, or the six-figure salary? Are you in an ungodly relationship and torn between staying and leaving? I know from experience how hard it is to let go of a soul tie that you've held on to for years. Or am I totally missing it? Have you ever accepted Jesus into your heart at all? Remember, a little of the wrong thing can spoil the whole mission. It is important to clear this question up within yourself.

I propose taking a minute to really seek the answer, repent if you need to, rededicate your life back to him if that is the conclusion you have drawn. At any rate, get it right with God. It would be great to take a pause here before reading part two of this workbook. Really seek the Lord and ask God to search your heart.

Scripture Reference

"You were running a good race. Who cut in on you to keep you from obeying the truth?

Galatians 5:7

Let's Work it Out!

Whew! This chapter was tough. A large amount of self -evaluation. Take this time to reflect and always refer to this workbook when it looks gloomy. In this Let's work it out section, free style and answer the questions I asked you within the chapter. Ask God to reveal to you the areas that are hindering you. Jot them down, pray and fast to shut your flesh down so that you can hear God clearly with no distractions. Remember, use the Word of God, which is the Sword of the Spirit! You can start with these scriptures:

John 3:16

Gal 5:7

Romans 10: 9-10

Romans 6:23

Romans 3:23-24

Acts 3:19-20

God Loves you!

Study each scripture above, one-by-one, and take notes of what God is revealing to you through scripture (use the additional notes section at the back of this workbook).

PART TWO

ARE YOU PREPARED?

SELF-CARE, ARE YOU READY BROTHERS? ARE YOU READY SISTERS?

Chapter 5
Personal Wellness

Do you bathe? I caught you off guard, didn't I? Don't get offended. This is a legitimate question. Do you know how many people suffer from depression in the world? Do you know how many suffer in silence? Neglecting personal hygiene is one of the many signs that someone may be depressed. Many Christians struggle with depression and other sensitive issues that are rarely discussed openly. So, when I ask you, did you bathe? It is merely to jerk you out of your stagnation and alert you that you are human and it's okay to have bad days. Just don't stay there. Get up and take a bath! Take care of yourself! I am rooting for you! You can do this.

Let's be true, many of us have let our personal care lag for whatever reason. But I am here to encourage you to change this not so much for others but for your own self esteem. The way we view ourselves can have either a positive or negative impact on our mental health. All of us may need additional help during our life span. So, if you need a mental break or therapy, pursue it. Taking care of yourself includes your mental health. As a man thinks, so is he. In observation, many of our behaviors follow how we view ourselves. Treat yourself well so that you can be well.

Men, your appearance is everything to a woman. Always leave your house like you are posing for a picture for a multimillion-dollar marketing package. Make sure you put yourself together well, shave nicely, apply lotion, use deodorant, clean your teeth, and trim those nose hairs. Let me give you a hint. The way you smell when you wear cologne will light a woman's eyes and spark her attention. She will smile all the way home. Most importantly, do a breath test before you approach anybody. In fact, brushing your teeth, using mouthwash, mints, candy or whatever can help curb bad breath. This should be a daily good practice. Most of all, don't neglect face-to-face appointments with a dentist. If you don't have insurance, research, or find free exams, call some colleges who have dentistry on campus and see if you can get a free exam. Do something! There is no excuse. This may sound harsh to some, but do you know how many people smile in your face and talk about your stink breath or your teeth behind your back? So, get it done.

Keep in mind as children of the highest God, we should not look like or dress simply off the opinions of this world, but we should look like we are blessed. How dare we abuse this body. I conducted some research to gain insights into why men often avoid seeking professional help or healthcare. An article in The American Journal of Men's health discussed the societal perception of male gender roles and its influence on men's willingness to seek healthcare. Kwon et al. (2023), In a study conducted, it was observed that men experiencing depression reported facing criticism and being called names when they expressed their struggles in social or workplace settings.

I want to encourage you today. If you have experienced name calling and criticism in your past on your health journey, I am sorry for every negative word spoken to you.

You are strong.

You are important.

You matter.

Your mental health matters.

Your voice matters.

You are needed.

You are wanted.

You are the righteousness of God.

Please keep up with your healthcare, no matter what.

Just in case you did not know, there are care gaps that every primary care office should screen you for. These gaps alert the physician if you are on target or not on your wellness journey. For example, men starting at 45 years old need to have a prostate and colorectal screenings, especially if there is a history of cancer in your family. I know we have the faith in God that He is our healer. However, let us try to at least gain wisdom and understanding and take a preventative stance. Get to know your bodies.

I would like to emphasize that during my research, screening rates in the past revealed Black adults are higher at risk for colorectal cancer than our Caucasian counterpart (Shah et al., 2022). Based on the same article, a task force recommended screening for colorectal cancer should be done for individuals aged 50 to 75. In addition, further research using the National Library of Medicine revealed in the same literature that less than half of Hispanic men were up to date with colorectal cancer screening, followed by Asian men (Shah et al., 2022). So, my single brothers, please get up to date on your colorectal screening and prostate exams. Prostate exams typically involve a digital rectal exam. Warning! The doctor will use a gloved and lubricated finger to examine the prostate wall through the rectum. Additionally, there will be a laboratory examination called the Prostate Specific Antigen (PSA) test. An elevated PSA level is abnormal and could be a sign of prostate cancer. Make sure you prioritize your health, please. These conditions are just some examples and are not limited to the ones mentioned in this workbook.

In addition, as a reminder, single Christians are to refrain from premarital sex. However, if you should do so, please protect yourself and your partner. If at any time a sexually transmitted disease (STD) occurs, please adhere to all treatments, and tell those who you may have encountered immediately.

Note to the reader: This workbook does not condone or promote premarital sex or judge you if you have indulged. Please repent. Treat yourself well so that you can be well.

Ladies.

Ladies.

Ladies.

My fellow sisters.

I did not leave us out. So, let me ask you this. Did you take a bath today? Yes, I had the audacity to ask you the same question. I would like to reiterate how important mental health is all around. One must not neglect those days when everything is going haywire. Take a pause and a reset. While I don't want to sound repetitive, it's important to mention that neglecting personal hygiene can be a sign of depression. Seeking professional help and securing a healthy mentality is a great reward. You owe it to yourself to have a healthy mind. Ladies, many of us are not just single, but single parents, caregivers, aunties, and grandmothers. Women, for some time, have been holding the weight of families on our shoulders. There is no time for crying or taking a break. We think that if we do so, the whole family will fall apart.

Say this with me.

They will not die if I say "No."

Sometimes there must be a "No" in your spirit without guilt. While weighing yourself down for others, others are having fun enjoying life and you are beat down and can barely move. The same things mentioned for our brothers applies to the women as well. Ladies, our hygiene needs are on a whole different level. We need to address key areas daily. Sometimes the information must be raw for some ladies to get it. One of our assets is the vagina and daily care, sometimes more than that is needed. We must get to know our bodies and not ignore them when something is not smelling right. Do not get me wrong, this is not to shame anyone, but unbelievably, there is a condition known as bacterial vaginosis (BV). When you notice an odor or itching down there, it indicates that something is off the scale. A gynecologist should perform a test to diagnose the condition. Researchers have studied BV and have found that it results from an imbalance of good and bad bacteria in the vaginal area. The Centers for Disease Control (2021) noted that there is no evidence of how sex causes BV, but also revealed it is associated with sexual activity and can increase chances of getting a sexually transmitted disease (STD). However, it is the PH of a female that has been triggered. A normal PH is between 3.8-5.0. The more acidic the better, which helps fight infections from occurring, which means the PH needs to be less than 7.

People often confuse BV with sexually transmitted infections (STIs) that have similar symptoms, such as Trichomonas (a sexually transmitted disease). Whenever there is a discharge from the vaginal area, that should give the female pause. One of the major symptoms is a fishlike smell. Woman of God sometimes BV occurs after a menstrual cycle, using douche products or anything that could upset the flora. Keys to remember, where cotton crouch underwear, do not wear tight-fitting pants/shorts that smash your vaginal area, no room to breathe and it breeds yeast. Try to use unscented soap if that is an irritant for your vaginal area. It would be a clever idea to use vaginal PH user-friendly products.

Wash it.

Wash it and wash it.

Please find a primary care physician and a gynecologist and keep up with your appointments. One being a yearly pap smear. If sexually active, please get evaluated at least every 3-6 months. As previously stated to the male audience, it is worth reiterating to the female audience that individuals who are single, especially those who follow the Christian faith, should refrain from premarital sex. However, if you should do so, please protect yourself and your partner. If at any time a sexually transmitted disease (STD) occurs, please adhere to all treatments, and tell those who you may have encountered immediately.

Note to reader: This workbook does not condone or promote premarital sex or judge you if you have indulged.

Please repent and treat yourself well so that you can be well.

Before moving on to oral hygiene, let's look at an issue the affects women over forty and that is menopause. Menopause occurs when a female no longer has her period and is typically observed in ages over forty-five. There are some variabilities as all women are not the same. However, this is just what menopause means. A woman's knowledge of potential changes that could occur in her body as she continues to live is also imperative to her mental health. Women's lack of knowledge about menopause and insufficient training of healthcare providers to support them can cause depression and anxiety. What do I mean by this?

A study shows that women under forty and over forty had little instruction about menopause and that their medical providers did not have enough training to educate them (Bisma et al., 2023). Here is my guess: that there is a possibility the male doctors dismiss this part of women's health. Unbelievably, menopause comes with so many challenges. Hip pain, lack of energy, and hot flashes, just to name a few. There are multiple medical conditions and issues that affect women's health. This workbook presented the most common ones noted in society. One other screening, women should maintain and that is the monthly self-check of one's own breasts. Your GYN will do this on exam, however as a female, taking your health into your hands is so important. Schedule your yearly mammogram or sooner if there has been a diagnosis of breast cancer in your family history. Mammograms are a part of maintaining female wellness. Please do not neglect this out of fear. Early detection results in a better life expectancy.

There seems to be a fantasy world created in the minds of people because it eludes the reality of how male and female bodies differ. It was determined some discussions needed to be exposed in this workbook as there will be adult men and women reading this tool who may have misjudged their previous partner's health conditions. Men need to be aware of the challenges women face as they advance in age. Just as women need to be aware of the challenges men face, such as erectile dysfunction (ED). This discussion will become more evident when you become married. This can affect your sex life with your spouse if not discussed beforehand. Prior knowledge will provide time to produce other alternatives properly in case the devil comes in and tempts your marriage bed.

Women lose estrogen which supplies the bones, ovaries which affect a woman's vaginal lubrication abilities. So, men, before you marry, get to know what changes a woman's body will go through. Will you stand by her even if the problem may not be about you? Personal wellness for the women includes oral care, just like our male counterparts. The same thing applies to women as well. See your dentist and get your gums checked. So many of us are walking around with bad breath, which could be related to the health of our gums. Make it a daily practice to care for your teeth. Appearance and attitude go hand in hand for the sisters. You act how you look. Okay, let me be transparent. When I get my hair done, honey, I have a diva like attitude. And a certain twist of the hips versus when I am having an unruly hair day, where the hair just will not lay right. Let us practice exhibiting a good attitude, smiling and cheerful even if you do not feel like it. Walk as if you are fearfully and wonderfully made. Put on that red lipstick, that nice outfit, walk like you are on the runway. Command attention when you enter a room without ever having to say one word.

You got this.
Go girl.

Our appearance is everything. Your mood will change when you begin to see yourself through God's eyes. My brothers and my sisters take time out of your busy day to treat and pamper yourselves.

You deserve it.

Remember my motto.

Treat yourself well so that you can be well.

Okay ladies, I am about to hit a sore spot again. Did you clean your house today? Are your clothes everywhere from the night before when you could not decide what you were going to wear to a party? Are the same dishes in the sink from three nights ago. Are the clothes you washed still in the washing machine or the dryer? Which one? Do you see any brown boys in your house? Don't pretend like you don't know what that means.

Roaches.

Do you have any?

Will your guest be afraid to use your bathroom?

There is no need to expand this topic out. Just clean your house. Think about it, say you are married. Do you want that man to step over uncleanness on the floor just to get into the house? I am just saying, get rid of that junk. Give it away if you are not using it. Many of us are holding on to stuff we cannot use and cannot fit into anymore. Walking into a clean house changes your mood for the better.

Treat yourself well so that you can be well.

One ultimate point is this chapter applies to both men and women. It is never okay to abuse someone. Whether verbally, physically, emotionally, or financially. This is unacceptable on all levels. Men, if you are the abuser, seek help and I say the same to the female. If someone is abusing you, seek help immediately. There is no time to waste here! Remove yourself and, if you have children, remove them from danger as well. I know this is easy for me to say, but I am a child who grew up in this type of situation. Now the laws are so much better than back in the seventies. Seek shelter in your city and state. I have provided the National Domestic Violence hotline phone number in the back of this book.

Scripture Reference

"Dear friend, I pray that you may enjoy good health and that all may go well with you, even as your soul is getting along well."
(NIV The Woman's Study Bible, 3 John 2)

Let's Work it Out!

1. Men, did you schedule your screenings yet? If this applies (age 50-75) For those who do not fit this age group, have you secured a primary care physician to maintain your health and close care gaps?

_____

_____

_____

_____

_____

_____

_____

2. Write down your personal views regarding your own health. How are you going to maintain your healthy habits?

_____

_____

_____

_____

_____

_____

_____

3. Mental health is important to maintaining a balanced life. Address head on mental issues you have been experiencing. Write them down. If you are on medications, write them down and the last time you took them. When was your last follow up appointment if you had a provider? How many appointments have you missed and why? Seek professional help. Seek your Pastor's for help.

_____

_____

_____

_____

_____

_____

4. For those not-so-good days, ask for a phone call or a virtual visit where you do not have to come out of the house.

_____

_____

_____

_____

5. Ladies, when was your last mammogram?

_____

_____

_____

_____

_____

_____

6. Reminder to check your breasts. If you have pain, drainage, or feel a lump, please contact your healthcare provider immediately! (Use these lines to write if necessary)

_____

_____

_____

_____

_____

_____

7. Contact the National Breast Cancer Foundation, INC (972) 248-9200 for informational resources. Write your questions beforehand.

_____

_____

_____

_____

_____

_____

8. Who is your dentist? Write down any issues with your oral care? Do you know there is a such thing as oral cancer?

_____

_____

_____

_____

_____

_____

_____

_____

_____

Chapter 6
Deliverance....The Real Work

Deliverance is key to maintaining a Christian believer's lifestyle. Find a church home that leads you by the Trinity: God the Father, God the Son, and God the Holy Spirit. Visit churches until God reveals the right place of worship to you. Attend church services where you will find strength in numbers. Attend as many Bible study and Sunday school sessions as possible to gain knowledge and understanding of the ways of the enemy. Once you choose to follow Jesus, stick with it. Remember, if you fall, the Lord will pick you up. Keep getting up.

To live a life of freedom, we must prune and purge certain areas of our lives. Once sin and soul ties become evident in the lives of people, there must be a time of deliverance. Once saved is not always saved. If an individual has fallen, repenting is not enough. That person must turn away from that sin but can encounter resistance and find themselves back in the same bondage. This part of the chapter is especially important for your growth and preparation while waiting for the gift exchange of single to married. Transparency with the Lord, seeking his face and allowing him to examine your heart is key to battling strongholds in your life. For instance, engaging in sexual sin can lead to aggressive spiritual attacks from spirit spouses and if you are married, the influence of this demonic entity can cause a lack of desire towards your partner. These demons by name are called Incubus and Succubus where they come and sleep with you during the night, where you move in the bed as if you are having a sexual encounter. No one likes to address this, but it is real.

Acts such as watching pornography, watching ungodly sexual content on TV, and listening to demonic music. Once that vision enters your spirit, it attempts to take over, causing you to have appetites you did not have before. The enemy uses tactics to bring a thought to your mind. A memory. Here is an instance where you must be strong enough to call on God, the father, the son, and the Holy Spirit to help to cast down that imagination. Take care of these unfruitful appetites now.

This kind goes not out but by prayer and fasting, and it may take your pastors, intercessors, and deliverance fasting to combat this enemy. While preparing for your mate in the waiting phase, take the time to denounce and divorce every act of participation with the enemy and his emps. As God gives you remembrance, call out every sin and denounce them one by one. Keep in mind this is not a quick session. This may take some time. Stay connected to your church pastor and leadership. Stay in your word, worship, and praise. We aim to close every door the enemy may try to gain access to. Keep in mind that when you do this, the enemy will try to circle around to see if he can still coerce you with the same sin.

For my sisters, other examples can be something so small, like keeping that lingerie in your drawer that you used for Joe; not realizing it is an attachment to the old you. Ladies, you cannot use this lingerie in your new marriage. This lingerie is associated with a past sin and must be destroyed. Brothers, that picture tucked deep in your wallet is causing a covenant that will come between you and your future wife. Get rid of it. Have you healed in your heart from that last relationship?

With every ungodly relationship, there are some forms of attachments, such as pictures, clothing, and gifts. Ask yourself, are you truly ready to be free or is the materialistic side of you so attached to this soul tie? All must be destroyed. Keep nothing that causes a remembrance or an open door to your past. Point number one, if it is still in your possession, it is an indication that you plan to go back. Consider this point: if a person or thing is keeping you from having a relationship with God and causes you to act in disobedience, then this is a stronghold you must conquer before marriage. Promiscuity, binge drunkenness, drugs, and living a riotous life is against God. These acts will eventually destroy you. Every act you are not delivered from can seep into relationships you are trying to build. People will be affected by your decisions. Once you are Christ's, there are benefits that come with the inheritance, one being deliverance. *(Mark 7:26-27)*. We must wear our armor every day to stand against these evil times. Do the work on yourself, work out your salvation before you marry.

I Decree and Declare

I am free from sin.

I am free from darkness.

I am free to worship.

I am free to praise.

There are no more chains keeping me bound.

I am healthy.

My mind is healthy and at peace.

My soul is rested.

My body is healed.

I am the righteousness of God.

I shall live and not die.

I am delivered.

"For our struggle is not against flesh and blood, but against the rulers, against the authorities, against the powers of this murky world and against the spiritual forces of evil in the heavenly realms."

Ephesians 6:12

Let's Work it Out!

This work it out section is for you personally. Call out those things that have you bound up with the enemy. Seek guidance for deliverance prayers from your pastor. *Psalm 51* should be in your daily prayer routine.

Deliverance Prayer

Father God, I acknowledge you as my Lord and savior and I know Jesus is your son who died for my sins, rose again on the third day and is now sitting on the right hand of you making intercession on my behalf. Lord, against thee have I done this evil in thy sight. Have mercy on me, blot out my transgressions, and wash away all my iniquities. Purge me with hyssop, wash me so that I may be whiter than snow. Create in me a clean heart and renew the right spirit within me. Lord, I divorce and denounce any affiliation with the devil and his helpers. I make you my Lord and savior as I realize I belong to you and you have purchased my life through your Son, Jesus.

Deliver me, oh Lord, that I may be free to serve you, worship you with unstained hands. I wish to worship you in the beauty of your Holiness. Deliver me from evil, deliver me from this stronghold of disobedience, lust, perversion, unclean heart, and spirit. Deliver my mind from bad thoughts,

Thank you, Jesus, for Delivering Me!

Chapter 7

Are You Ready to be a Husband?

Men, ask yourselves, am I really ready for a wife? Then ask yourself, am I ready to deal with whatever she comes with? I mean, what if she does not come in a full beauty package? You know, the package that was fathomed in your mind even before you met her.

What if you do not see what you created in your mind, are you ready for singleness for the rest of your life or are you ready to reform your way of thinking of what a wife is supposed to look like, act like or sound like? Have you considered the heart of a woman versus the looks of a woman? Pretty on the outside, but cannot count, read, or manage a household. I am just saying to be sure who you are choosing.

These are the questions that need to be tackled because if you come across the person you have envisioned in your mind, for example, with a body measurement of 36-24-36, and she turns out to be 44-49-70, then what? So, before you think you are ready, really ponder on what would you do if the frame of the image in your mind becomes shattered. Do you shatter her and leave, or do you love unconditionally? Meaning not based on looks, but on God and purpose, for better or for worse. Are you just fishing and not planning to catch? Because if you are not ready to catch, do not even go to the pond.

There was a brief discussion in the personal wellness chapter of this workbook that hit on some health conditions women experience. Not all women may experience the same signs and symptoms of menopause, however what if your spouse does? What are you willing to do to help her through the ordeal? Support or Abort, I ask? How should you care for your spouse? Are you willing to care for her through the advanced stages of life or will the midlife crisis hit you and deceive as an excuse to find someone younger? Be prepared to prevent the destruction of lives. Time on this earth is not without limitation. Now let us get to the meat of this chapter.

Men, do you have a job? Are you prepared to take care of the needs of both you and your wife? Have you considered what if you both have children? Have you counted the cost? What about discipline? What kind of discipline and who is going to decide the punishment? Are you good with money? Will you have a problem if she makes more money than you? What happens if she desires a prenuptial agreement? What factors would make or break the deal? Will it be 50/50 with you or is this negotiable? Do you have a plan?

My number one question is, are you ready to be a husband? Have you studied the word of God to see what he expects of you as a husband? *Genesis 2:18* reads, "The Lord God said it is not good for a man to be alone. I will make a helper suitable for him." Is uniting with a suitable helper what you are looking for? Marriage is no game. It is a covenant between two people. Marriage is not for the selfish. Both partners are expected to contribute to the relationship, with one partner occasionally giving more than the other. This leads me to the topic of submission.

One misconception relating to submission seemed to have pointed to being the sole responsibility of the women. I must reveal the word of God refers that the submission is one to another. Why? It is to reverence our Lord and Savior. I used to think God was on the side of the man and where was his care or concern for the female. The belief that women should always be submissive was forcefully imposed on us, repeatedly hammered into our minds, leading to a rebellion among many women. Obeying and submission were like curse words to the women of God. The men stood firmly on this and were so aggressive about it. This was my personal experience, so I dare not offend anyone, however it was not until I studied the word of God for myself where God was not a respecter of persons. He confirmed through his word in Ephesians 5:21 that we are to submit one to another.

Ok fellas, do you have a will to change your mindset to conform to the ways of God? Remember, this singles workbook is all about doing the work while waiting. Exploring the concept of submission, submitting, etc., in the Bible, I came across an extremely reliable resource, known as The Strongest, Strong Exhaustive Concordance. The word submitting is hypotasso (Greek number (5293) means to put in subjection, subject, subordinate, to submit, to put under, made subject, obedient, subdued, subdue under obedience (Strongest, Strong Exhaustive Concordance, 2001. p. 5323). What are your thoughts about these definitions, my brothers? How do you feel about submitting to your future wife, based on these definitions? I conclude both parties must be accountable. Man of God, are you ready to love your wife to be? *Ephesians 5:25a* reminds us that husbands should love their wives, just as Christ Loved the church and gave himself up for her to make her holy. Christ died for us all. He gave of himself by standing in the gap for our sins. Therefore, the husband should always cover for his wife and not deal harshly with her.

There is a specific divine order of the family, Christ, husband, wife, and then the children. There has been controversy regarding the order of the family. My brothers, are you ready to lead like

Christ or are you an Ahab? Ahab let Jezebel rule him and decide on his behalf. What are you ready to do for your family to be? What comes before your wife? Your ability to hear and be led by God, determines it. How can you lead her without a relationship with God? Where are you leading her to? Do you have a vision for your family? Are you ready to leave and cleave? Mama and others should not be interfering or have a say in your marriage. If advice or counseling is an option, seek professional assistance, because mama and auntie and them will have you in divorce court. You may have been ready to leave your mother and father and cousins and sisters to cleave. However, that doesn't mean that they were ready. Are you prepared to stand up for your wife against your family? Remember, Jesus gave himself.

God has a benefit for men when they find a wife. He receives good pleasure from the Lord *(Proverbs 18:22)*. Do you want the favor of God? My brothers in Christ, I leave you with one last thought. If you had a daughter, would you recommend someone like you to be her husband?

"Husbands. Love your wives, just as Christ Loved the church and gave himself up for her to make her holy, (26) cleansing her by the washing with water through the word (27) and to present her to himself as a radiant church without stain or wrinkle or any other blemish but holy and blameless."

Ephesians 5: 25-27

Let's Work it Out!

1. Write out your expected role as a husband. Compare it with the word of God. Be prepared to use this one day in premarital counseling. Write a vision.

_____

_____

_____

_____

_____

_____

2. What qualities are you looking for in a wife? And do you possess these same qualities?

_____

_____

_____

_____

_____

_____

_____

3. This chapter contains many loaded questions. Did you find yourself having second thoughts about becoming a husband? If so, use this time to explore, ask questions, talk to your Pastor about your thoughts. Are they realistic or thoughts of fear?

_____

_____

_____

_____

_____

_____

4. Let's do an experiment and write down your findings in this section. The assignment is to observe two married couples. Did you observe anything that may deter you from wanting to be a husband? What were the positive and what were the negative aspects? This exercise will help you see how other marriages operate. (Hint: not every marriage is the same or has the same ingredients)

_____

_____

_____
_____
_____
_____
_____

5. How do you oversee frustration or bad days? Do you throw things or hit people? In other words, how do you manage conflict?

_____
_____
_____
_____
_____
_____

6. How can you protect your wife from outside interference?

_____
_____
_____
_____
_____

Chapter 8
Are You Ready to be Found Ladies?

The scripture reads that he who finds a wife, finds a good thing, and obtains favor from the Lord. Are you a wife? Because being a wife is something you are already walking in when your God given spouse is looking for you. Do you possess the qualities of a wife? Let's look at the book of *Proverbs. Chapter 31*, to be exact, and it starts around verse ten. The scripture reads, "who can find a virtuous woman? What kind of character do you possess? Are you someone who tends to be bossy, unruly, and dishonest, or are you more of a kind, loving, understanding, and easily approachable person who can form deep connections? Will you treat him kindly and avoid causing him any harm? What benefits will your spouse receive from being married to you? Women, take this question seriously and reflect upon it in *Proverbs 31:11*. Is his heart secure in your hands?

Ask yourself, will I be able to manage what he gives me? Think of your current state as a single woman. Are you managing the things of God? How is your credit, your health? Is your house clean? When your future spouse comes home, what will he come home to? Chaos or peace? Will he be on the rooftop or in his king's corner? *(Proverbs 21:19)* Be sure you are what you are praying for to GOD. Most importantly, can you cook? Whatever skill you are lacking, start taking classes now. Be proactive. There is so much free social media about how to cook, clean house and even how to wash clothes. Cook small dinners, experiment, practice. Ladies, have you thought about what kind of job you're working on right now? Are you willing to contribute to the household needs or are you expecting to have everything done by your spouse? Are you truly ready to be a helpmate for him in all areas, or are you lazy?

What about future years, his health and advanced age? Are you ready to work with your spouse if he has erectile dysfunction (ED)? Will you seek another to satisfy that need or will you support your husband in finding other alternatives for your marriage? How should you care for your spouse? It is important to plan out these things in advance. What if your parents or his parents need shelter, time, or recuperation in your home versus a nursing home? Are you against this? Is this a deal breaker? For what exactly are you ready to be found doing? Ask yourself if you had a son, would you recommend someone like you to your son as a wife?

"… and the wife must respect her husband."

NIV The Woman's Study Bible, 2018

Ephesians 5:33b

Let's Work it Out!

1. What does a wife look like to you? Study *Proverbs 31:10-31*. Make a note of key points while studying these scriptures.

_____

_____

_____

_____

_____

_____

2. Lists areas of improvements you observe in your life that could hinder your marriage.

_____

_____

_____

_____

_____

_____

_____

3. What did your attitude look like the last time you did a self-check? How do you deal with conflict? Do you throw things or yell?

_____

_____

_____

_____

_____

_____

4. The Delilah mentality stripped Sampson of his strength as a man he laid in the lap of a woman who could not keep his heart safe. _(Judges 16:6-17)_ Take time to evaluate previous relationships. Point out anything in your personality that stripped him of his dignity and strength. Work on self. (Hint: sometimes it's the smallest thing).

_____

_____

_____

_____

_____

_____

Words of Encouragement

What an amazing journey this has been.

I would like to thank you for choosing my workbook.

I designed this with my brothers and sisters of Christ in mind.

Singles stand your ground while you are on your journey of waiting.

I pray that on your most lonely days; you remember God will never leave you or forsake you and

that he is perfectly designing someone just for you.

Resources/References

Bible Gateway. 7Jul (2022).

https://www.biblegateway.com/passage/?search=Isaiah+56%3A5&version=KJV

Centers for Disease Control and Prevention. (2021). Sexually transmitted Diseases;

Bacterial Vaginosis. CDC Basic Fact Sheet. Last reviewed 5 Jan 2022.

https://www.cdc.gov/std/bv/stdfact-bacterial-vaginosis.htm

Fortune, D. & Fortune, K. (1987), (2009). Discover Your God-Given Gifts. Chosen

Books a division of Baker Publishing Group.

Hsu, A. (2022). Singleness: A Biblical Perspective. Discipleship Journal, 108, 36.

KJV

Kwon, M., Lawn, S., & Kaine, C. (2023). Understanding men's engagement and

disengagement when seeking support for mental health. American journal of

men's health, 17(2), 15579883231157971.

Merriam-Webster. (n.d.). Eunuch. In Merriam-Webster.com dictionary. Retrieved April

13, 2024, from https://www.merriam-webster.com/dictionary/eunuch.

NIV Women's Study Bible Full Color Edition Copyright @2018 by Thomas Nelson

Shah, S. K., Narcisse, R., Hallgren, E., Felix, H. C., & McElfish, P.

A. (2022). Assessment of Colorectal Cancer Screening Disparities in U.S. Men

and Women Using a Demographically Representative Sample. Cancer Research

Communications, 2(6), 561-569. https://doi.org/10.1158/2767-9764.CRC-22-0079

Tariq, B., Phillips, S., Biswakarma, R., Talaulikar, V., & Harper, J. C. (2023). Women's

knowledge and attitudes to the menopause: a comparison of women over 40 who were in the perimenopause, post menopause and those not in the peri or post

menopause. BMC Women's Health, 23(1), 460.

Strong, J. (2001) Fully Revised and Corrected. Kohlenberger, J. & Swanson, J The

Strongest Strong's Exhaustive Concordance of The Bible Larger Print Edition.

(2001).

Important Numbers

National Domestic Violence Hotline 800-799-7233 (last verified April 18, 2024)

National Suicide Hotline 1-800-273-8255 (last verified April 18, 2024)

Please call 911 for any emergencies!

About the Author

Tanya Marayne is a professional nurse who also has a passion for writing books, plays, and lyrics. She established her own company, DAR J PRODUCTION LLC and, launching her inaugural singles workbook designed for adults, brings her immense joy and anticipation.

You can connect with Tanya via email at: tmarayne@darjproductions.com

Additional Notes:

Made in the USA
Columbia, SC
08 July 2024

38259153R00059